Knowing Your O'pen BIC Sailboat

▲

Philip C Freedman

Published by Philip C Freedman

ISBN-13: 978-1490344522
ISBN-10: 1490344527

Printed in the United States of America

CONTENTS

INTRODUCTION

So when I first saw an O'pen BIC sailboat in early 2013, I knew that after fifty years of sailing, this was something I had to be involved in. It takes a lot for me to get excited about sailboats, but this was it.

Wow!

Having been a college sailing coach, high school sailing coach, author of six sailing books, sailing sports writer, speaker, commentator, and having had an Olympic Campaign (1988 Olympic Trails, Star Class, skipper), America's Cup Campaign (1992 Skipper/CEO Betsy Ross America's Cup Group) made me more than appreciate the O'pen BIC sailboat - youth sailing at its best.

Learning just got easier. In one of the biggest junior sailing makeovers in the last seventy-five years and with today's technology BIC Sport has come up with a breakthrough for the junior sailing enthusiast. BIC Sport has simply put the fun and excitement back into junior sailing with the O'pen BIC junior sailboat.

A meteor has hit junior sailing and the dinosaurs have disappeared. Junior sailing has become of age. In one of the biggest sailing upgrades in history, the O'pen BIC junior sailboat has leaped over the competition and has taken junior sailing to the next level. The future of junior sailing is here today and it's here with the O'pen BIC sailboat. Welcome to the 21st century of youth sailing.

This book contains information on your O'pen BIC sailboat. You will find a breakdown of all the parts for the O'pen BIC along with sailing, racing and simply knot definitions. You will also find a glossary of sailing terms that will need as you advance..

My goal is to make sailing a successful venture not only for the team or club, but for each student wanting to learn how to sail. This book will give you a good foundation for going to the next level.

I made the flash cards simple, with pictures of every item, to make it easy to understand what you are looking at. Also the sailing glossary is I believe one of the best and easiest to understand. Inside this book you will find is the best way to get familiar with the basic terms of the boat, rigging, sails and equipment.

Please remember that you can have some good times here. Times that you will always remember, but you will also have the fun of sailing, a skill that you will love and enjoy forever.

Enjoy. You deserve it.

—Philip Freedman

Lined up and ready to go in the 2013 O'pen BIC Hi-Wind Challenge that was held during the finals of the Louis Vuitton Cup for the 34th America's Cup in San Francisco, California. This event was the largest crowd in history to witness a youth sailing regatta.

2013 O'pen BIC Hi-Wind Challenge
The AC OPEN "Un-Regatta"

O'pen BIC

August 17-18, 2013

At the America's Cup Village - Marina Green

Sailboat Specifications

LOA *(Length Overall)*	**9 feet**
MAINSHEET	**18 feet - 5/16**
BEAM *(Width)*	**3 feet 9 inches**
HULL WEIGHT	**99 pounds**
MAST HEIGHT	**12 feet 10 inches**
MAINSAIL *(Rig Monofilm 4.5)*	**48 square fee**

The O'pen BIC is a single handed sailboat designed for youth sailors. Developed by Vitali Design, the boat was first launched in 2006. It is an International Class, as recognized by the International Sailing Federation (ISAF), and as of 2014 8,000 boats have been built.

The thermoformed polyethylene hull is self-draining. In the event of a capsize or shipping water by some other means, the water simply flows down the angled floor of the cockpit and out of the open transom.

The two part, 12 foot 10 inch, O'pen Bic mast is made from a fiberglass epoxy composite. The boom is made from aluminum which hold a 48 square foot sail made from K.Film - Polyester, with full length battens of adjustable tension. The foils are manufactured out of composite epoxy.

O'PEN BIC

The hull of the O'pen BIC was designed with fun sailing as the priority. It is a modern boat where the hull is as open as possible, thereby leaving the helmsman completely free to move around and trim the boat to any wind and water conditions. When hiking, the large sides allow the sailor to set-up comfortably with his/her feet in the straps without placing any unnecessary stress on the body. The totally open and sloping cockpit means that there is absolutely no water in the boat either during sailing or just after a capsize. A relatively hard chine design was chosen for the bottom shape of the hull. Used by numerous modern boat architects, this design offers an excellent compromise between performance and stability. When reaching or broad-reaching, the boat accelerates quickly to planing speed. When close-reaching, the boat sets on its chine and has excellent performance up wind.

The rig includes a fully-battened, 4.5m² mono-film sail with mast pocket, similar to that of a windsurf sail.

Rigged on an epoxy mast, the sail has been designed with an open leech to give sailors maximum control and performance in windy conditions.

List of O'pen BIC World Champions

2014 Travemünde, Germany
Gold   ?
Silver   ?
Bronze   ?

2013 Lake Garda, Italy
Gold   Zampiccoli Federico (ITA)
Silver   Gallinaro Guido (ITA)
Bronze   Paula Garcia Igual (ESP)

2012 Miami, Florida, United States
Gold   Nick Muller (USA)
Silver   Andre Reguero (PRI)
Bronze   Hugo Stubler (FRA)

2011 Ascona, Switzerland
Gold   Hugo Stubler (FRA)
Silver   Giacomo Ferrari (ITA)
Bronze   Vianney Bergot (FRA)

2010 Martinique, French Caribbean Islands
Gold   Brice Yrieix (FRA)
Silver   Vianney Bergot (FRA)
Bronze   Simon Jestin (FRA)

2009 Medemblik, Netherlands
Gold   Kevin Bergers (NED)
Silver   Vianney Bergot (FRA)
Bronze   Bart Lambriex (NED)

2008 Carnac, France
Gold   Denis Tassone (BRA)
Silver   Constaza Seguel (CHI)
Bronze   Santhiago Sampaio (POR)

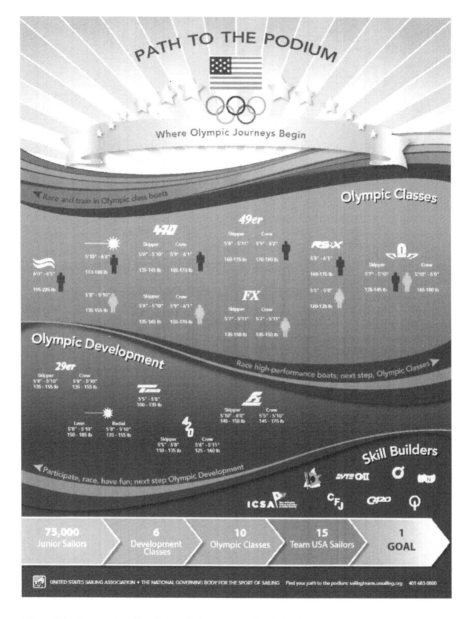

The **"Path to the Podium"** is a wonderful chart that shows the many different skill levels of diggy sailing. You will see that the O'pen BIC sailboat is displayed under skill builders. What a great way to start your youth sailing.

Welcome to the 21st Century of Youth Sailing

▲

PHILIP C FREEDMAN

PARTS OF THE SAIL

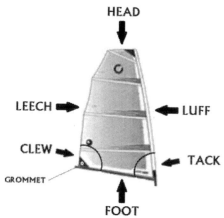

HEAD of the sail
The *head* of the sail is located at the very top of the sail. The O'pen BIC's sail is a square headed sail.
FOOT of the sail
The *foot* of the sail is the bottom of the sail, and runs the length of the boom.
LUFF of the sail
The *luff* of the sail is the leading edge of the sail and runs up and down the mast from the head of the sail to the foot of the sail.
LEECH of the sail
The *leech* of the sail is the trailing edge of the sail running from the head of the sail to the foot of the sail.
TACK of the sail
The *tack* of the sail is located on the lower forward corner of the foot and the luff of the sail as indicated in the diagram above.
CLEW of the sail
The *clew* of the sail is located on the lower aft corner of the foot and the leech of the sail as indicated in the diagram above.
GROMMET
There is one *grommet* located on the sail, the one grommet is located in the corner of the clew of the sail which is used to attach the outhaul which pulls in on the foot of the sail to trim.

BOW / STERN

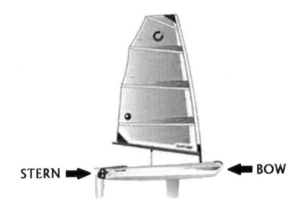

The **bow** is the front of the boat. On the O'pen BIC there is also a **front hull protector** and a **towing handle** for easy use.

The **stern** is the aft portion of the boat. This is where the **top and bottom rudder mounts** are located that are used to attach the **rudder.** This is also where the **leash cord** that is attached to the **rudder** attaches to the **hull.**

PORT SIDE - STARBOARD SIDE

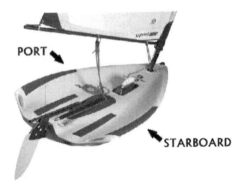

The **port side** of the **hull** is on the left side of the **hull** when looking forward. The **starboard side** is on the right side of the **hull** when looking forward.

RUDDER

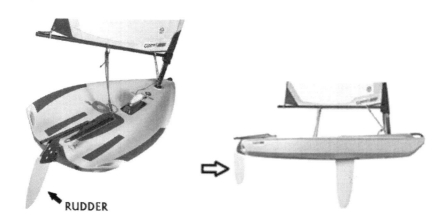

RUDDER

The O'pen BIC *rudder* is a very simple, but highly designed system that is attached to the *stern* of the *hull*. The *rudder* is attached to *top rudder mount* and a *bottom rudder mount* that is located on the *stern* of the *hull*.

Rudder Mount Bottom   **Rudder Mount Top**

After you have attached the *rudder* to the *rudder mounts* it is very important to attach the ***rudderblade leash*** to both the *hull* and the *rudder*.

THIS IS IMPORTANT AS THE RUDDER DOES NOT FLOAT

Rudderblade Leash

1

The *rudder* has four additional parts:

- *Tiller*
- *Tiller Extension*
- *Red Control Line*
- *Green Control Line*

MAST / BOOM

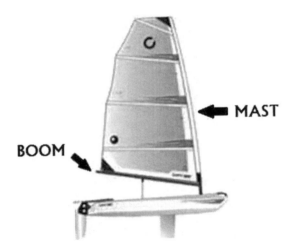

The *boom* is one piece and is made of **aluminum.**

The *mast* is two pieces that attach together and is twelve feet ten inches tall. The *sail* slides over and down the *mast*. The *mast* is made of **fiberglass-epoxy**.

DAGGERBOARD

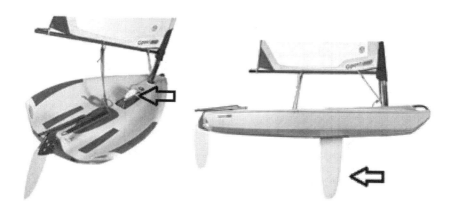

You can do everything with your *daggerboard*. Located in the forward center portion of the *hull*, the *daggerboard* allows stableization of the *hull* and ability to point while going upwind. As in an airplane, the thrust, drag, lift, and weight, the *daggerboard* should be up in your perferred position while going downwind for less drag which slows the boat speed down.

Also, you will notice red horizonal lines on the *daggerboard*. This allows you to remember your desired setting when going upwind or downwind. Remember always keep your *daggerboard retaining loop* attached around your daggerboard.

3

 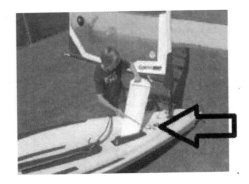

Daggerboard Retaining Loop

Always keep your *Daggerboard Retaining Loop* attached around the daggerboard at all times.

SAIL BATTENS

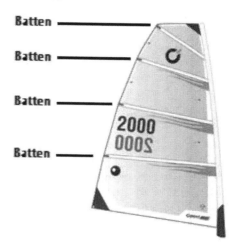

There are four **battens** in an O'pen BIC **mainsail**. The **battens** go from the **luff** to the **leech** on the **mainsail**.

BOW-LINE / PAINTER

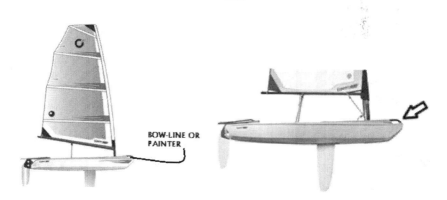

BOW-LINE OR
PAINTER

The bow-line/painter is attached to the **towing handle** located on the **bow** of the **hull**. This line can be used to attach the boat while on the **boat dolly**, attach to a cleat while at the dock, or to be hand held to ready the boat at the dock or boat ramp.

MAINSHEET

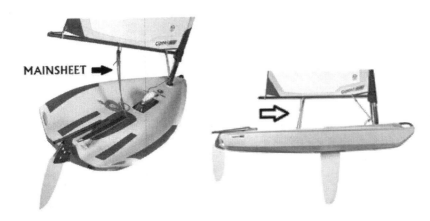

The *mainsheet* controls the tension of the *mainsail*. The *mainsheet* is 18 feet long with a width of 5/16's. and is attached to the boom. Always remember to tie a *figure eight knot* at the end of, or bitter end, of your *line* to pervent the *mainsheet* line from pulling thru your *ratchet block* when the boom is fully extented.

The *mainsheet* slides thru the *mainsheet ratchet block* which than attaches to the *deck mount.*

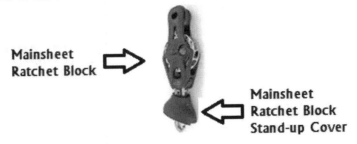

Mainsheet
Ratchet Block

Mainsheet
Ratchet Block
Stand-up Cover

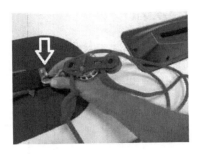

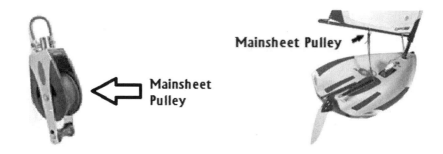

The **mainsheet pulley** is the block that the **mainsheet** goes thru to control the **booms** movement.

OUTHAUL

The **outhaul** is a system that attaches to the **grommet** at the **clew** of the **sail**. The **outhaul** system controls the tension of the **foot** of the **sail**. You can adjust the tension depending on weather conditions.

DOWNHAUL CUNNINGHAM PULLY & HANDLE

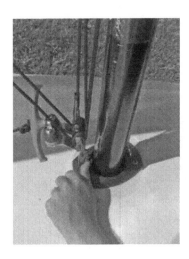
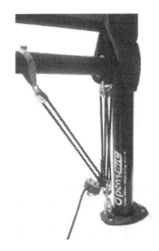
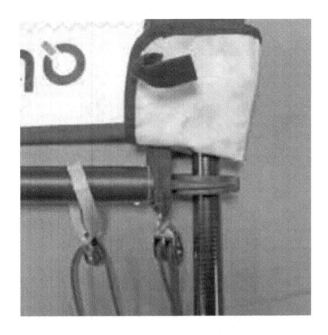

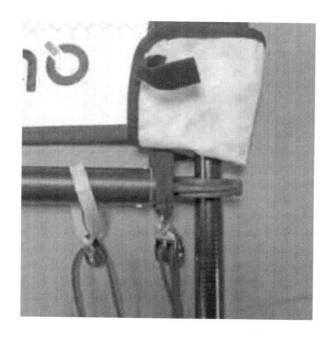

The ***cunningham tackle*** (6 threads and cleat) associated with the ***boom vang / boom safety attachment***, allows you to trim efficiently the tension of the sail.

DRAIN PLUG

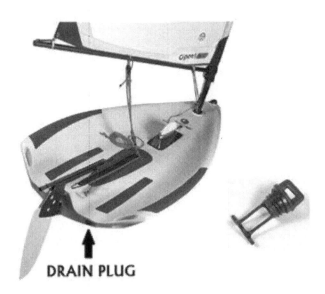

DRAIN PLUG

The ***drain plug*** is more important than you think. First, it keeps water out of the ***hull***. Second, when you get the boat out of the water, drain any water that may have accumulated out of the ***hull***. At six pounds a gallon, that's a lot of weight to slow you down, plus it will throw off your boat balance. Third, when the ***hull*** is in storage, keep the ***drain plug*** open. When the ***drain plug*** is open, it keeps pressure equal on both the inside and the outside of the ***hull***. This prevents the ***hull*** from getting soft by contracting or expanding. It's always nice to have a spare ***drain plug*** in a parts ***plastic***-toolbox.

Plastic – Spare Parts Toolbox

BOAT DOLLY

The **boat dolly** is used to make it easy to transport the boat to and from the water for storage and or transportation.

How do I assemble my O'pen BIC boat dolly in less than :60 seconds

1. Attach frame part 1 to frame part 2. (one snap)

11

2. Attach frame part 2 to frame part 3. (another snap)

3. Attach wheel 1 to frame. (would you believe, another snap)

How to Assemble Your O'pen BIC Sailboat

▲

1. Take the **sail**, **boom**, and **mast** parts out of the sail bag.

2. Unroll the **mainsail** and stretch it out flat.

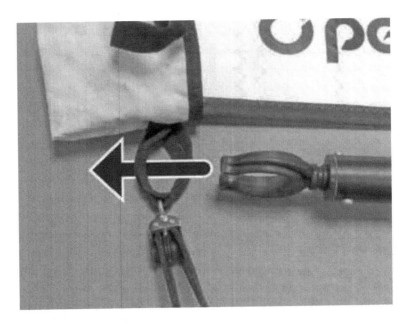

3. Slide the **boom** (**boom fork** end first) thru the **tack strap** of the **sail**.

4. Attach the **outhaul** to the **grommet** at the **clew** of the sail.

5. Slide the **mast** up the **luff** portion **(mast pocket)** of the sail thru the **boom fork** of the **boom**.

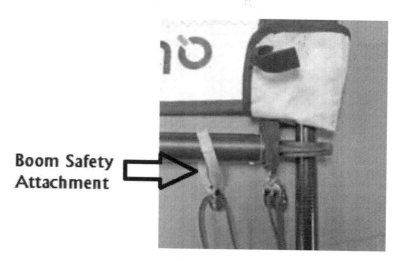

Boom Safety Attachment

6. The assembled portion should look like this.

7. Drop the **mast** down into the **mast support** of the hull.

8. Tighten the **downhaul.**

9. Make sure that the *lines* are not twisted.

10. The finished product should look like this.

11. Attach the **snap shackle** of the **mainsheet ratchet block** to the **deck mount** on the hull.

11. Pull on the **cunningham handle** and **cunningham pulley** to tighten.

12. Attach the *rudder* to the *rudder mounts* on the *stern* of the *hull*. Make sure that both the upper and lower *rudder mounts* are attached properly

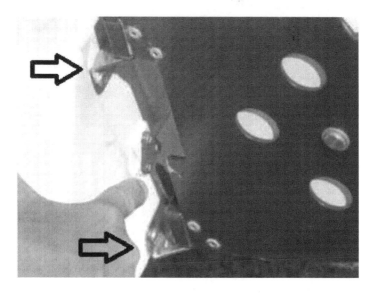

13. Make sure both ends of the *rudder* are attached to the upper and lower *rudder mounts.*

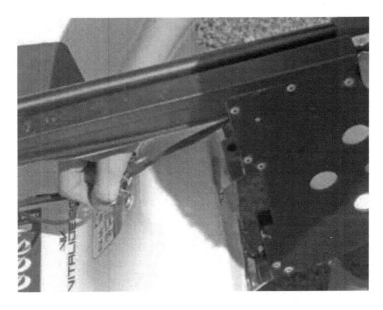

14. Tighten the red and green lines to your desired positions and tighten the lines on their *clam cleats*.

15. Make sure the *leash cord* is attached to both the *rudder* and the *hull* of the boat. You don't want to lose your *rudder* as the **RUDDER WILL NOT FLOAT**.

16. Slide the *daggerboard* thru the *daggerboard retaining loop* and down thru the *daggerboard case top.* Always have the *daggerboard retaining loop* around the *daggerboard.*

Done!

PHILIP C FREEDMAN

How to Disassemble Your O'pen BIC Sailboat

▲

Disassembling the boat

- Start by taking the leash cord, rudder, and daggerboard off the boat.
- Undo the *mainsheet* and *cunningham*
- Remove the *mast* from the *hull*
- Remove / slide the *mast* from the *sail pocket* of the *sail*.
- Loosen the *outhaul* as to not stretch out the *foot* of your *sail*.
- Roll the *sail* up, leaving the *boom* attached to the *foot* of the *sail*. Leave all blocks and lines attached.
- Separate the two part *mast*.
- Roll everything together and slide back into the sail bag.

- Lift the *mast* from the *mast support* of the hull.

- Remove the **mast** from **mast pocket** of the **sail**.

- Roll the **sail** up keeping the **boom** attached.

- Slide back into the *sail bag* for easy storage.

PHILIP C FREEDMAN

Part List for an O'pen BIC Sailboat

▲

PHILIP C FREEDMAN

Parts of an O'pen Bic Sailboat

Hull Parts

Center Toestrap / Hiking Strap (about $19.95)
Ref: 53263

The *center toestrap* is attached to the *deck mount* and enables you to hike out of the boat for better boat balance.

Daggerboard Case Bottom (about $24.95)
Ref: 53266

The *daggerboard case bottom* is located on the bottom or underside of the *hull* and is attached to the *hull*.

Daggerboard Case Top (about $24.95)
Ref: 53265

The *daggerboard case top* is located on the top of the hull and is attached with eight screws. This is what the *daggerboard* slides into.

Deck Mount - Mainsheet (about $4.95)
Ref: 53262

The *deck mount* is what both the *center toestrap* and the *mainsheet ratchet block* are attached to.

Draining Bungs (bag of 10) (about $29.95)
Ref : 30978

Not a bad idea to have some spare *draining bungs* in you plastic tool box. You don't want to miss a sailing day because of one of these.

Eyelets (bag of 10) (about $24.95)
Ref : 30977

The *eyelet* is attached to hull to secure the *bungee daggerboard retaining loop.*

Front Hull Protection (about $49.95)
Ref: 53268

The *front hull protector* prevents damage to the *hull* when coming into the dock, transporting, or just sailing with other boats.

Front Towing Handle (about $14.95)
Ref: 52789

The *towing handle* is located on the *bow* of the boat and aids in the lifting, towing, and securing the *hull* to both the dock or *boat dolly.*

Mast Support – Bottom (about $14.95)
Ref: 53276

The bottom of the *mast support* is located below the top portion of the *mast support.* This piece allows for better support of your *mast.*

Mast Support – Top (about $14.95)
Ref: 53275

The top piece of the *mast support* is attached to the hull and allows easy installation of the *mast.*

Rudder Mount Bottom (about $14.95)
Ref: 53269

The *rudder mount bottom* is part of the two piece support system that is attached to the *stern* of the *hull* in *which the rudder is attached to the hull. The rudder mount bottom* also has a <u>*clip*</u> to lock the *rudder* in place.

Rudder Mount Top (about $14.95)
Ref: 53270

The *rudder mount top* is also part of the two piece support system that is attached to the *stern* of the *hull* in *which the rudder is attached to the hull.*

Rudder Retaining Clip (about $4.95)
Ref: 53271

The *rudder retaining clip* is a spring that holds the *rudder* onto the *pintle*. Should be replaced every couple of seasons.

Set of Pads Complete (about $59.95)
Ref: 31458

These black pads are attached on the top deck of the *hull* of the boat as an anti-skid to help prevent sliding on the desk.

Support for Draining Bung (about $4.95)
Ref: 53264

The support for the *draining bung* is attached to the *stern* of the *hull* and allows for easy screw in of your *draining bung.*

Adaptor Ring for Optimist Rig - (about $14.95)
Ref: 53347

This adaptor ring allows you, when inserted in the *mast support*, to use your Optimist Rig on the O'pen BIC *hull*.

Tiller Parts

O'pen BIC Tiller Extension Complete 70 cm (about $49.95)
Ref: 53312

The *tiller extension* is attached to the *tiller* of your *rudder*.

Rudderblade Leash (about 14.95)
Ref: 31563

The *rudderblade leash* is a safeguard that if the rudder comes off the hull it will not sink as the rudder **WILL NOT FLOAT.** <u>Always</u> keep the *rudderblade leash* attached.

Tiller Clam Cleat (x10) (about 24.95)
Ref: 31560

These *tiller clam cleat* allow you to secure both the red and green lines that lock in place the position of your *rudder*.

Tiller End Plug (bag of 10) (about $24.95)
Ref: 31558

The *tiller end plug* is a cap for the very end of the tiller and helps prevent it from damage.

Daggerboard Parts

Daggerboard Retaining Loop (about $9.95)
Ref: 53322

The *daggerboard* simply slides thru the *daggerboard retaining loop* and *daggerboard case top* into and thru the hull to secure the *daggerboard* in place.

Sail Parts

Allen Batten Tensioner for 3.8m2 North Sail (about $9.95)
Ref: 31545

The *batten tensioner* allows you to change the stiffness of your *battens* located in you sail depending on weather conditions.

Batten End Cap for 3.8 North Sail (about $4.95)
Ref: 31489

The *batten end cap* is located at the end of the *batten* by the *leech* of the *sail* and keeps the *batten* in place to prevent it from sliding out of the *sail.*

Batten Tension for 4.5 North Sail (about $19.95)
Ref: 31488

You can change the *batten tension* depending on weather conditions. Stiffer for high wind and loose for light wind.

Sail Batten North Sail (largest size) (about $19.95)
Ref: 31487

There are four *battens* in the O'pen BIC sail. All four are different sizes.

Vario Top Male Plug -North Sail (about $9.95)
Ref: 31490

The *top male plug* is at the top of the sail and slips into female plug (31326) at the top of the mast.

Mast Parts

Mast Plug Female – Top (about $4.95)
Ref: 31326

The female *mast plug* is found at the top of the *mast* and accepts the male plug at the top of the *sail*.

Mast Plug for Bottom of Mast Reinforcement (about $9.95)
Ref: 31386

The *mast plug* has two purposes. 1) Keeps water out of the *mast* and 2) works as a reinforcement to keep the bottom of the *mast* from damage.

Boom Parts

Boom Fork (about $24.95)
Ref: 31328

The *boom fork* is attached to the forward portion of your aluminum *boom*. The *boom fork* secures the boom with the *mast.*

Boom Safety Attachment (about $19.95)
Ref: 31319

The *boom safety attachment* comes as part of the complete *boom* and is used to attach the *line* that controls the *vang* adjustment on the boat.

Clew Hook (about $14.95)
Ref : 31329

The *clew hook* is attached to the *boom* and is used to adjust the *outhaul* on the *sail*. The *clew hook* attaches to the *grommet* on the *clew* portion of the *sail*. You can adjust the tension of the *outhaul* depending on weather conditions.

Cunningham Handle (about $14.95)
Ref : 31561

The *cunningham handle* is attached to the *cunningham pulley* shown below. This makes for an easy way to pull on the *cunningham*.

Cunningham Pulley (incl. rope & handle) (about $149.95)
Ref : 53289

This line controls the *cunningham.* With the *cunningham handle* (shown above) this pulley system provides easy adjustment of your trimming system.

Dyneema Link Ratchet Block (about $9.95)
Ref : 31546

The *dyneema link ratchet block* attaches the *mainsheet ratchet block* (31331) to the clip that attaches to the *deck mount* (53262).

Mainsheet Protection (about $19.95)
Ref : 51548

This is an unessential neoprene cover that protects your knees from where the *mainsheet* attaches to the deck.

Mainsheet Swivel Block Top - Pulley (about $49.95)
Ref : 31330

The *mainsheet pulley* is the top portion of the *mainsheet* that is attached to the *boom.*

Mainsheet Ratchet Block (about $149.95)
Ref : 31331

The *mainsheet ratchet block* attaches to the *deck mount*. The *mainsheet line* goes thru the *ratchet block*.

Mainsheet Ratchet Block Stand-Up Cover (about $9.95)
Ref : 31548

The *mainsheet ratchet block stand-up cover* goes over the *mainsheet ratchet block* and prevents your *mainsheet* from getting caught while sailing,

Mainsheet Rope 8mm red, 5.8m (about $29.95)
Ref : 31562

The *mainsheet rope* is eighteen feet long with a width of 5/16's. Don't forget to put a *figure eight knot* at the end of the line/sheet. The end of the line/sheet is called the bitter end.

Retainer Clip Ratchet Block (about $9.95)
Ref : 31547

The *retainer clip ratchet block* attaches the *dyneema link ratchet block* (31546) to the *ratchet block* (31331).

Accessories

O'pen Bic Boat Dolly / Trailer (about $349.95)
Ref : 31394

Easy to store and easy to transport makes the *boat dolly* great to have. Remember this assembles in less than two minutes.

O'pen Bic Top Cover (about $124.95)
Ref : 31377

Keep your hull dry and clean while storing your boat on a *boat dolly.* You can also store your *sail, mast, boom, rudder, daggerboard* under the top cover.

O'pen BIC Top Cover Deluxe NORTH (about $199.95)
Ref : 31633

This is the heavy duty version of the above *top cover.*

O'pen Bic Blade Bag- North (about $149.95)
Ref : 31630

This is the best way to protect your *rudder* and *daggerboard* and is simple to carry or store.

O'pen Bic Gear Bag – North (about $49.95)
Ref: 31632

You have to love the *gear bag.* This bag can be used for just about anything from sailing to school. You have to have one of these.

Rigs

O'pen Bic Rig Monofilm 4.5 – Complete (about $1299.95)
Ref: 11738

The rig includes a fully-battened, 4.5m² mono-film sail with *mast* pocket, similar to that of a windsurf sail.
(48 square feet of sail area)

Sail 4.5 m2; - Monofilm (about $499.95)
Ref: 53323

This is the monofile forty-eight square foot *sail*. Come with four battens.

Sail 3.8 m2; - Dacron (about $449.95)
Ref: 53447

This is a smaller version of the O'pen BIC *sail*. This sail is made of Dacron and still comes with the battens. Some people enjoy sailing the smaller *sail*.

Sail 4.5 m2; Dacron NEW (about $549.95)
Ref: 53781

This is the same size as the fully-battened, 4.5m² mono-film *sail* with *mast pocket*, similar to that of a windsurf sail, but is made of dacron sail material.
(48 square feet of sail area)

Complete Mast (about $299.95)
Ref: 31375

The *complete mast* is made up of a two piece fiberglass-epoxy material that is twelve feet ten inches tall when attached together.

Complete Boom & Fittings (about $599.95)
Ref: 31315

The aluminum *boom* comes with *line, blocks, outhaul*, and your *cunningham* and *vang* system.

Rudder (complete) (about $449.95)
Ref: 31784

The *rudder* (complete) comes with the *rudder, tiller, tiller extension*, and green and red line that locks the *rudder* in your desired position.

Daggerboard (about $349.95)
Ref: 31785

The *daggerboard* is used to stabilize the boat while sailing and aids while pointing the boat upwind. There are three red horizonal lines on the *daggerboard*. This allows you to remember your desired setting when going upwind or downwind. Remember to always keep your *daggerboard retaining loop* attached around your daggerboard.

WINDEX / TELTAILS

Wind indicators are great to have and will help you determine the direction of the wind. There are *teltails* on both sides of the *sail.*

BOAT BALANCE / HIKING OUT

Hiking out is very simple and helps with boat balance. Simply side you feet under the *center toestrap* that is attached and you are on your way. Hiking out is not only easy to do, but a lot of fun too.

PORT TACK / STARBOARD TACK

PORT TACK

Being on a *port tack* means having the wind coming over and filling your sails from the *port side* of the boat.

STARBOARD TACK

Being on a *starboard tack* means having the wind coming over and filling your sails from the *starboard side* of the boat.

POINT OF SAIL

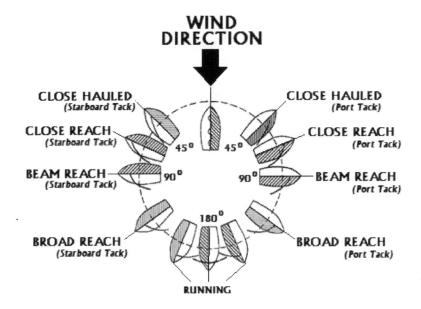

Luffing / Irons
This means going diirectly into the wind. This will slow the boat and is very useful when starting a race or coming back to the dock.

Close Hauled
The closest you can go into the wind, usually 45 degrees off the wind. Remember, when racing, the idea is to get from point A to point B.

Close Reach
Sailing between *close hauled* and a *beam reach*.

Beam Reach
Course steered at right angles to the wind.

Broad Reach
Wind is coming behind the boat at an angle.

Running
The wind is coming from directly behind the boat commonly called DDW (dead-down-wind).

SAMPLE - RACE COURSES

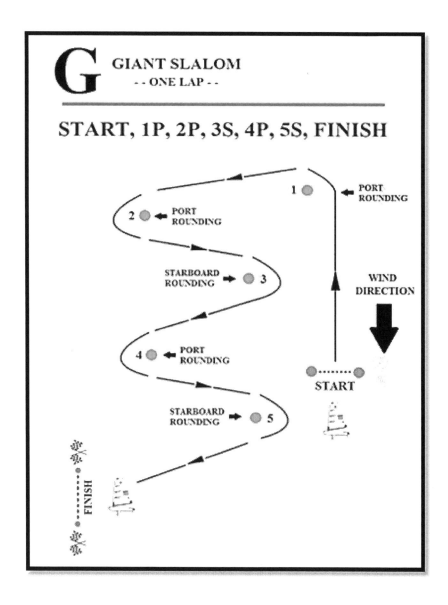

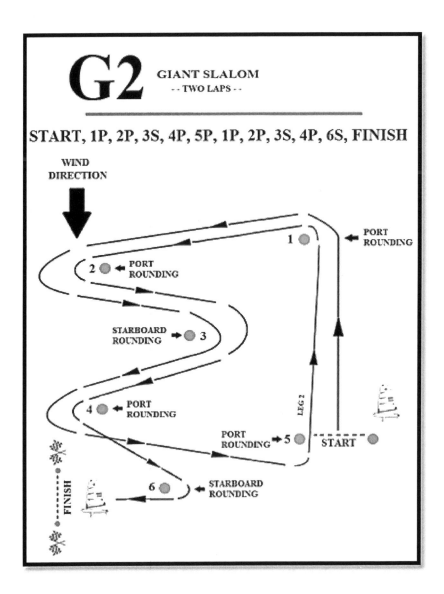

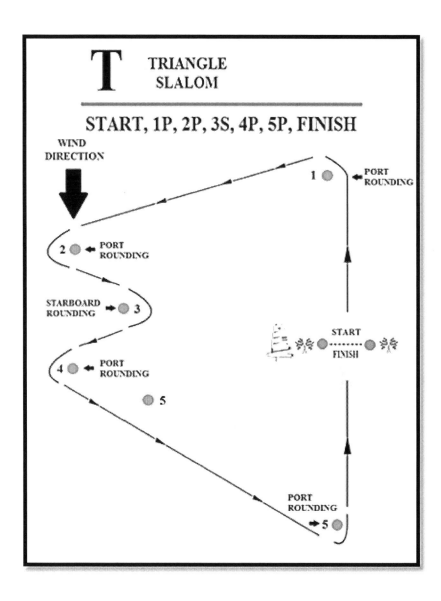

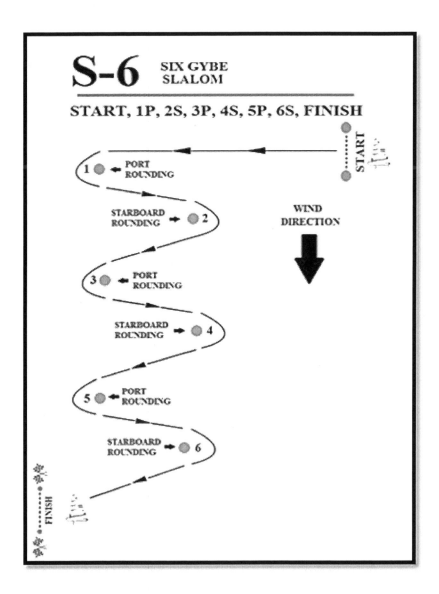

S-6 SIX GYBE SLALOM

START, 1P, 2S, 3P, 4S, 5P, 6S, FINISH

PLAYING IN THE SANDBOX

STARTING BOX

The sandbox is the starting area before the start of the race. I call it the sandbox because it's the place where you can either get sand thrown at you, or you can throw sand at you opponents. Stay in the sandbox and run the starting line from the committee boat to the flag and back. *Know that line and never be over the line early*.

Also run the course a little, if you have time. While running the port and starboard tacks, pick a point on the horizon on each tack and remember it. This will help you know when you are getting headed, which is when you're losing compass degrees.

Once in start mode, don't wander out of the sandbox. Stay in the action and make your presence known. Also remember that depending on the wind, if it's light, it takes more time to get to the starting line. I've seen boats with a minute to go <u>not</u> make the starting line on time, so gear your time accordingly.

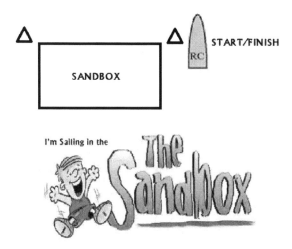

55

THE CHICKEN JIBE GYBE

Remember in the movie back to the Future when Michael J. Fox hated being called "Chicken". But eventually he smartened up – didn't take the dare and changed his future for the good. Well … sometimes in sailing it's equally as smart to not take the dare.

The safe maneuver is called the chicken jibe.

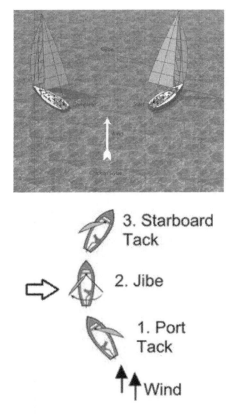

The chicken gybe (shown above) replaces a normal gybe in high winds

It's mostly done when the skipper is uncomfortable about the conditions for the gybe and most likely if the winds are high. High winds in a gybing maneuver can cause damage to the vessel rigging by the boom SLAMMING across too fast. In a normal gybe maneuver the boom slam effect can be reduced by pulling in the main sheet and letting it out as the boom comes over to the other side.

However, in high winds – 15 knots plus, if the boom is not let out fast enough, the wind on the main sail will round the boat up in to the wind and heel the boat way over and even capsize.

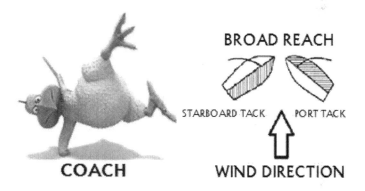

BROAD REACH

STARBOARD TACK   PORT TACK

COACH   **WIND DIRECTION**

So the best choice is the chicken gybe. The end result is the same. You are merely tacking the boat from a *broad reach* on one side over to a *broad reach* on the other side.

WHAT IS A KNOT

1 knot = 1 nautical mile per hour = 6076 feet per hour
1 mph =1 mile per hour = 5280 feet per hour

5 Knots = 5.8 MPH   25 Knots = 28.8 MPH

10 Knots = 11.5 MPH   30 Knots = 34.6 MPH

15 Knots = 17.3 MPH   35 Knots = 40.3 MPH

20 Knots = 23.0 MPH

Building a Six Boat O'pen BIC Storage Rack

▲

BUILDING A (6) BOAT STORAGE RACK

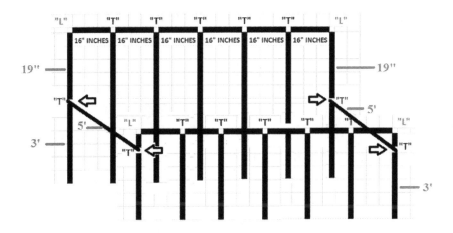

PVC Need List:

- (10) Ten Footers / PVC 2" inch = 100' feet
- (14) "T"s / PVC 2" inch
- (4) "L"s / PVC 2" inch
- PVC - Glue

Cut PVC lengths:

- (12)   16" inch / 2" inch PVC lengths
- (2)   6" inch   / 2" inch PVC lengths
- (5)   48" inch / 2" inch PVC lengths
- (4)   36" inch / 2" inch PVC lengths
- (5)   36" inch / 2" inch PVC lengths
- (2)   12" inch / 2" inch PVC lengths

Wood / Screws / Washers / Drill Bit:

- (6) 2" x 6" Ten Footers / Pressure Treated Lumber for Base

- (24) Washers

- (24) 3 ½ x 5/16" Lag Screws
  (Drill clean first, so it doesn't crack)

- 2 ½" inch Drill Bit
  (14) holes / hard to drill
  (pick out dry treated pieces)

ESTIMATED COSTS:

- (14) "T"s at $2.50 ea.   = $35.00
- (4) "L"s at $2.00 ea.   = $ 8.00
- 100' feet 2" inch PVC   = $80.00
- (6) Ten Footers - Wood   = $36.00

$159.00 Estimated

1. Start by cutting all the PVC parts to the indicated lengths shown.
2. Insert all the pieces together, but **<u>DO NOT GLUE !!!</u>**
3. Lay the assembled PVC rack on top of the treated wood and mark where you want to drill the holes for the PVC to go in.
4. Drill the holes. (This is not easy)
5. Place the assumbled PVC portion into the holes.
6. If you're happy with the fit, glue the PVC pieces together (or) make adjustments than glue.
7. FINISHED

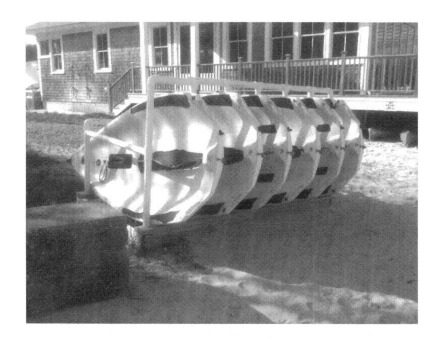

FOUR BOAT TRAILER EXAMPLE

PHILIP C FREEDMAN

Parts of the Sail

▲

Flash Cards

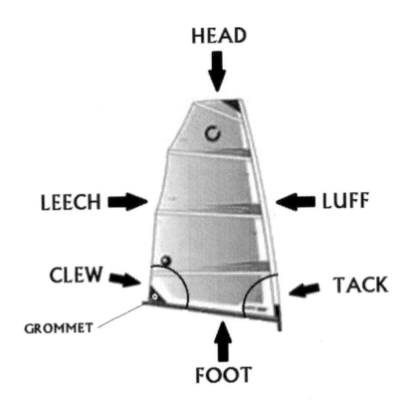

BATTEN

PARTS OF THE SAILS

CLEW

PARTS OF THE SAILS

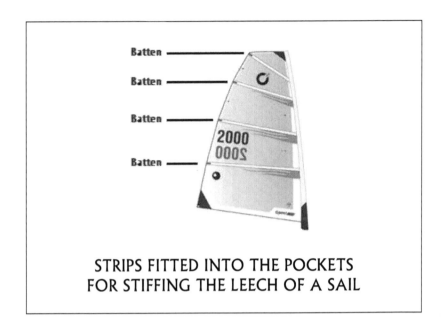

STRIPS FITTED INTO THE POCKETS
FOR STIFFING THE LEECH OF A SAIL

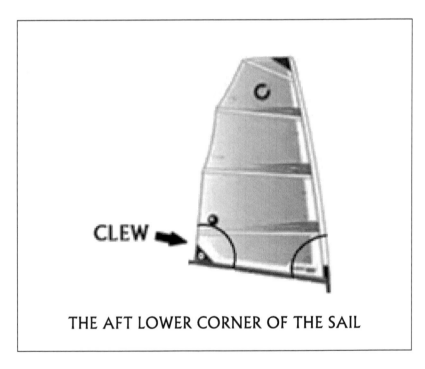

THE AFT LOWER CORNER OF THE SAIL

FOOT

PARTS OF THE SAILS

GROMMET

PARTS OF THE SAILS

FOOT

THE VERY BOTTOM PORTION OF THE SAIL

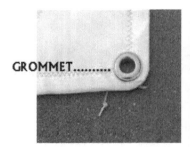

GROMMET..........

AN EYE IN THE SAIL IN WHICH TO PASS A ROPE

HEAD

PARTS OF THE SAILS

LEECH

PARTS OF THE SAILS

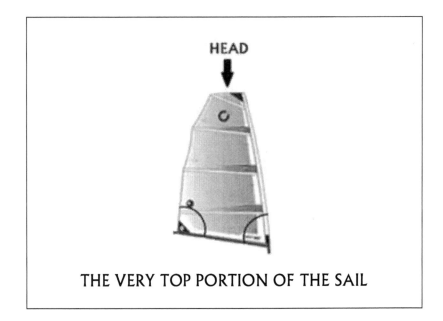

THE VERY TOP PORTION OF THE SAIL

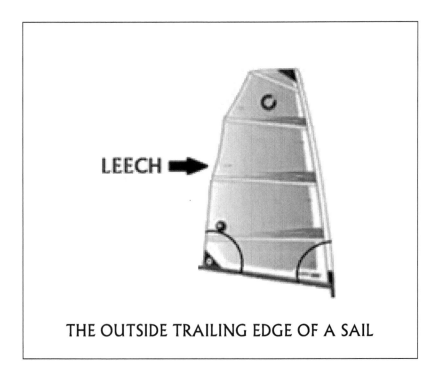

THE OUTSIDE TRAILING EDGE OF A SAIL

PARTS OF THE SAILS

PARTS OF THE SAIL

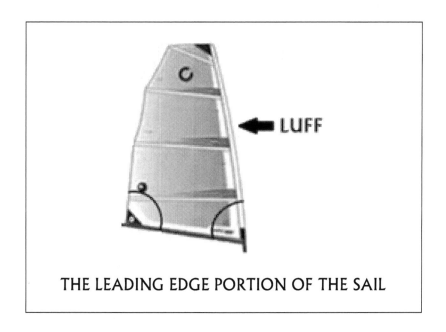

THE LEADING EDGE PORTION OF THE SAIL

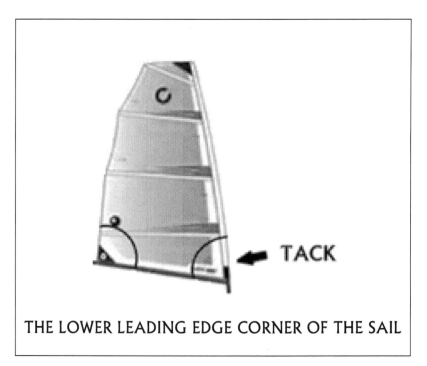

THE LOWER LEADING EDGE CORNER OF THE SAIL

Points of Sail

▲

Flash Cards

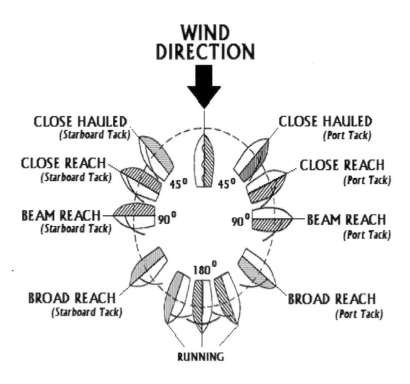

WIND DIRECTION

CLOSE HAULED
(Starboard Tack)

CLOSE HAULED
(Port Tack)

CLOSE REACH
(Starboard Tack)

CLOSE REACH
(Port Tack)

45°   45°

BEAM REACH
(Starboard Tack)

BEAM REACH
(Port Tack)

90°   90°

180°

BROAD REACH
(Starboard Tack)

BROAD REACH
(Port Tack)

RUNNING

BEAM REACH
POINT OF SAIL

BEAT
POINT OF SAIL

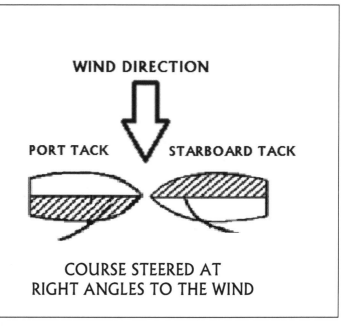

WIND DIRECTION

PORT TACK   **STARBOARD TACK**

**COURSE STEERED AT
RIGHT ANGLES TO THE WIND**

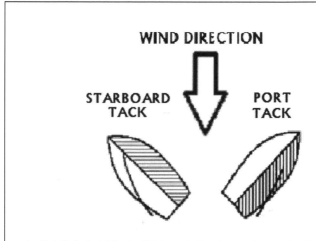

WIND DIRECTION

**STARBOARD
TACK**   **PORT
TACK**

**A SAILBOAT IS ON A BEAT WHEN THE BOAT IS
AS CLOSE TO THE EYE OF THE WIND AS POSSIBLE
ABOUT 45 DEGREES. WIND IS FROM AHEAD.**

BROAD REACH

POINT OF SAIL

CLOSE HAULED

POINT OF SAIL

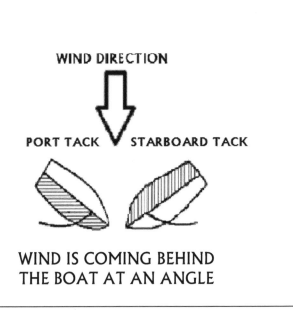

WIND IS COMING BEHIND
THE BOAT AT AN ANGLE

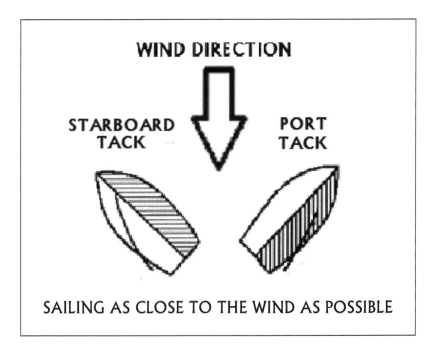

SAILING AS CLOSE TO THE WIND AS POSSIBLE

CLOSE REACH

POINT OF SAIL

HEADER

POINT OF SAIL

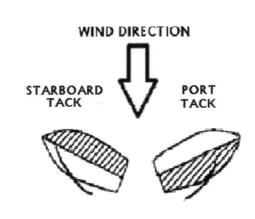

**UPWIND ANGLE BETWEEN
CLOSE HAULED AND A BEAM REACH**

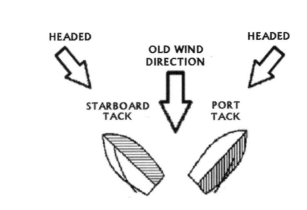

**IF YOU ARE ON A STARBOARD TACK
AND THE WIND SHIFTS TO THE LEFT, THEN
YOU ARE HEADED, YOU CAN'T SAIL AS HIGH**

IRONS

POINT OF SAIL

JIBE

POINT OF SAIL

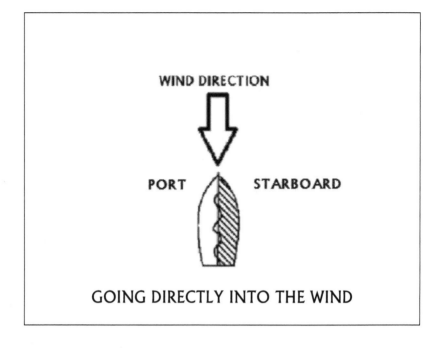

GOING DIRECTLY INTO THE WIND

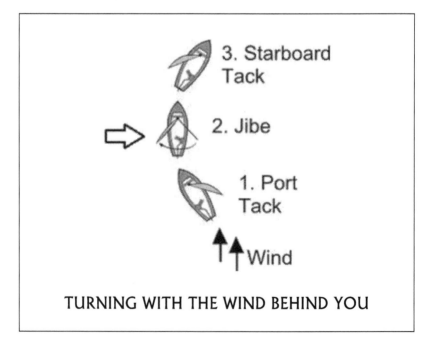

TURNING WITH THE WIND BEHIND YOU

LIFT
POINT OF SAIL

PINCHING
POINT OF SAIL

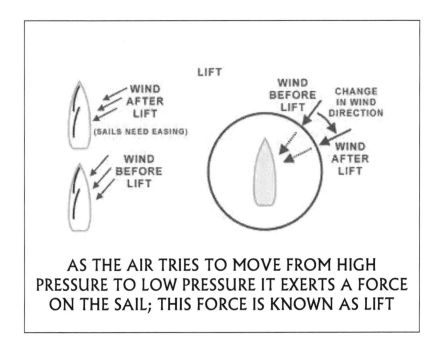

AS THE AIR TRIES TO MOVE FROM HIGH
PRESSURE TO LOW PRESSURE IT EXERTS A FORCE
ON THE SAIL; THIS FORCE IS KNOWN AS LIFT

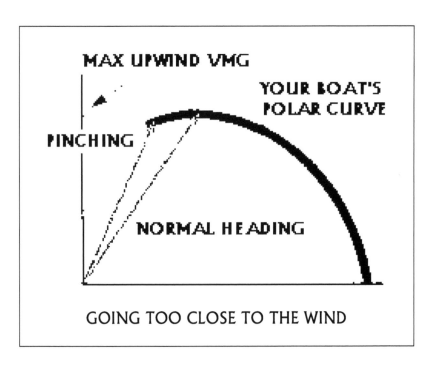

GOING TOO CLOSE TO THE WIND

PORT TACK
POINT OF SAIL

PUFF
POINT OF SAIL

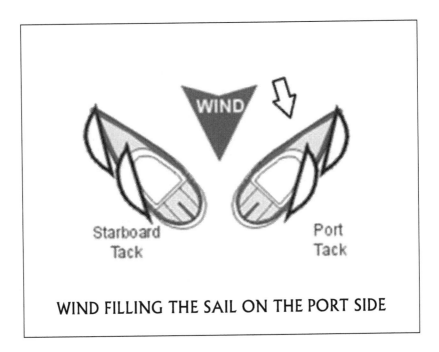

WIND FILLING THE SAIL ON THE PORT SIDE

WIND THAT IS COMING TO YOU OFF THE WATER

RUNNING

POINT OF SAIL

STARBOARD TACK

POINT OF SAIL

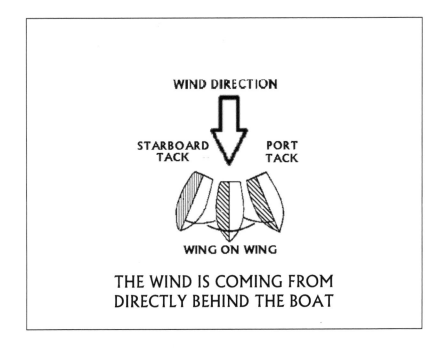

THE WIND IS COMING FROM DIRECTLY BEHIND THE BOAT

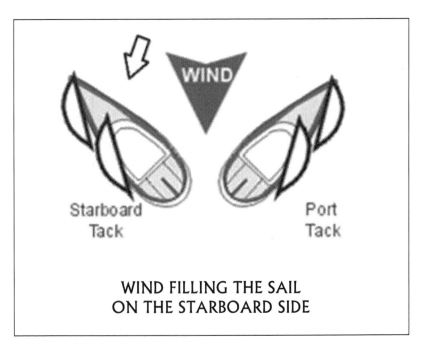

WIND FILLING THE SAIL ON THE STARBOARD SIDE

TACKING

POINT OF SAIL

Wind

 3. Port
Tack

 2. Passing through
the eye of the wind.

 1. Starboard
Tack

CHANGING COURSE GOING INTO THE WIND

Racing

▲

Flash Cards

PHILIP C FREEDMAN

COUNTDOWN WATCH
RACING TERMS

LAYLINE
RACING TERMS

A REVERSE TIME PIECE
USED FOR RACE STARTS

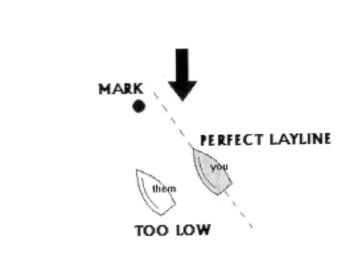

LINES UPON WHICH YOU CAN SAIL CLOSE
HAULED AND JUST MAKE IT AROUND THE MARK

MARKS
RACING TERMS

PORT ROUNDING
RACING TERMS

INFLATED ANCHORED COURSE INDICATOR

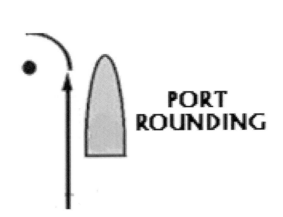

PORT
ROUNDING

MARK STAYS ON THE LEFT
SIDE OR PORT SIDE OF THE BOAT

STARBOARD ROUNDING
RACING TERMS

TRIANGLE COURSE
RACE COURSE

MARK STAYS ON THE RIGHT SIDE
OR STARBOARD SIDE OF THE BOAT

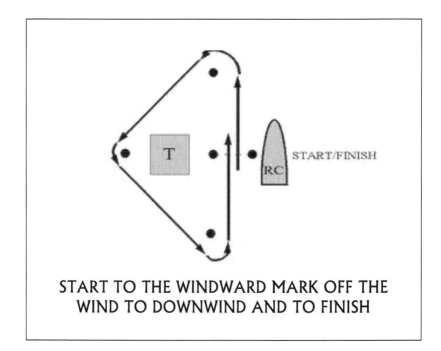

START TO THE WINDWARD MARK OFF THE
WIND TO DOWNWIND AND TO FINISH

WHISTLE STARTS
RACING TERMS

WINDWARD LEEWARD
RACE COURSE

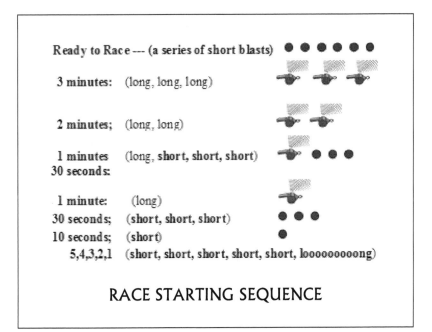

RACE STARTING SEQUENCE

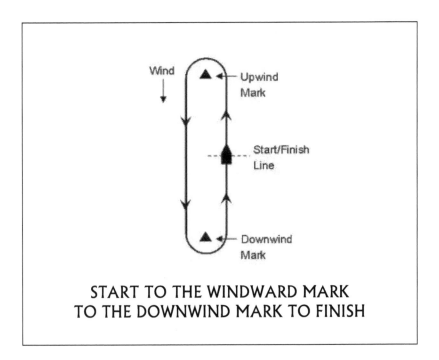

START TO THE WINDWARD MARK
TO THE DOWNWIND MARK TO FINISH

Simple Knots

Flash Cards

PHILIP C FREEDMAN

BOWLINE

TYPE OF KNOTS

FIGURE EIGHT

TYPE OF KNOTS

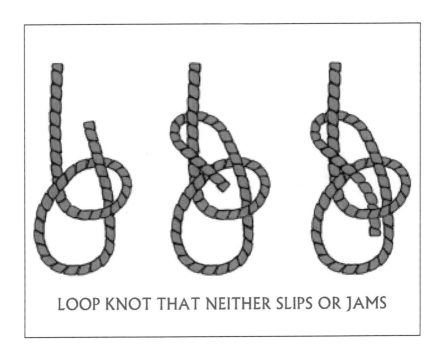

LOOP KNOT THAT NEITHER SLIPS OR JAMS

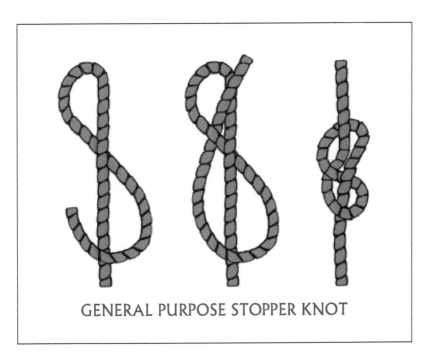

GENERAL PURPOSE STOPPER KNOT

SQUARE KNOT

TYPE OF KNOTS

CLOVE HITCH

TYPE OF KNOTS

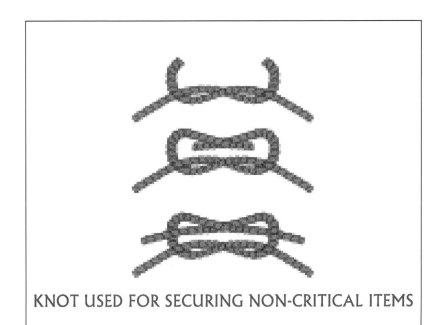

KNOT USED FOR SECURING NON-CRITICAL ITEMS

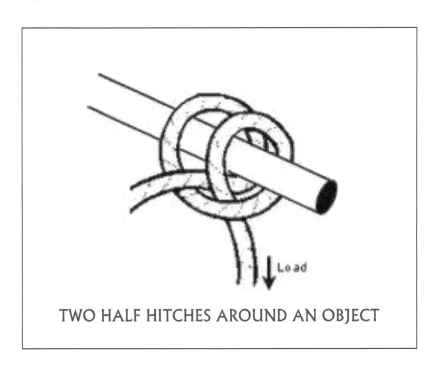

TWO HALF HITCHES AROUND AN OBJECT

Sailing Terms

142 GLOSSARY SAILING TERMS

Backstay – A backstay is the stay that runs from the top of the mast to the stern of the boat. The backstay is specifically designed to prevent the mast from blowing forward.

Bail – It is used to attach things to a spar. The bail is often attached to the boom or mast via a through bolt or rivet

Bailer - A plastic device to remove water from the boat. You can also washing machine soap bottles cut open.

Batten - Flexible strips of wood or plastic, most commonly used in the mainsail to stiffing the leech portion, or roach, so that it will not curl.

Beam Reach – Course steered at right angles to the wind.

Beat – When a sailboat is on a beat the boat is as close to the eye of the wind as possible about 45 degrees, wind is from ahead.

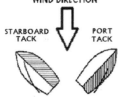

Block - A block is a single or multiple pulleys. One or a number of sheaves are enclosed in an assembly between cheeks or chocks. In use a block is fixed to the end of a line, to a spar or to a surface.

Boat Cover – Keeps the sun, water, and dirt out of the boat.

Boat Dolly - Enables you to walk or transport the boat into the water or to be moved or stored.

Boat Trailer – Enables you to two a boat with your car or truck. This trailer holds three boats. It can be pulled behind a car or truck for easy transport. Masts, booms, and boat dollies are also carried on this type of boat trailer.

Boom – A spar that attaches to the mask with a gooseneck or rope.

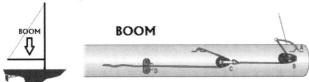

Boom Vang - A system used to hold the boom down, particularly when boat is sailing downwind, so that the mainsail area facing the wind is kept to a maximum. Frequently extends from the boom to a location near the base of the mast. Usually tackle- or lever operated.

Bow - The forward or front part of the boat and or hull.

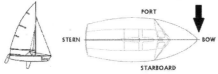

Bow Bumper - The bow bumper protects the bow of the hull from damage such as bumping into the dock or other boats.

Bowline Knot – Loop knot that neither slips nor jams

Bow Line (or) Painter - The bow line or painter is a line that is tied to front or bow of the boat. It can be used to tow the boat or tie it to the dock. In the picture below it is used to secure the front of the boat to the dolly so the hull stays in place

Broad Reach – Wind is coming behind the boat at an angle.

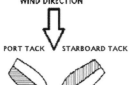

Capsize – Is when a sailboat is turned over on it's side.

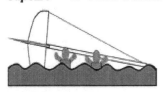

Centerboard - Is a retractable keel which pivots out of a slot in the hull of a sailboat which allows the centerboard to operate in shallow water, to be trailered, or retracted on downwind legs.

Centerboard Gasket – Are commonly found on racing dinghies, and are made of Mylar sheets. The idea is to limit the amount of water that can come into the hull by securing the seal between the hull and the centerboard.

Chicken Jibe – You are merely tacking the boat from a Broad Reach on one side over to a Broad Reach on the other side.

Cam Cleat - A cam cleat is a spring loaded device for securing rope but is easy to release. A cam cleat is in which one or two spring loaded cams pinch the rope. A jam cleat is where the line is pinched in a v-shaped slot.

Clam Cleat – A bracket used to temporary attaches and adjust sheets, lines, and ropes

Clevis Pin - The clevis pin is similar to a bolt, but is only partially threaded or unthreaded with a cross-hole for a cotter pin.

Clew of the Sail – The lower aft corner of a three sided sail

Close Hauled – Sailing as close to the wind as possible.

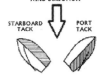

Close Reach – Upwind angle between close hauled and a beam reach.

Clove Hitch – Two half hitches around an object.

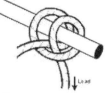

Compass – Used to show direction and bearings.

Countdown Watch – A reverse time piece used for race starts

Cunningham / Downhaul - In sailing, a Cunningham or Cunningham's eye is a type of downhaul used on a Bermuda rigged sailboat to change the sail. Pulls down the tack of the sail to change the sail's shape

 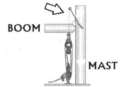

Dock Cleat - Wooden or metal fitting usually with two projecting horns around which a rope may be made fasten.

Dock Line – Line in which to secure a boat.

Draft – The vertical distance between the waterline and the bottom of the boat.

Drain Plug – A plastic screw on piece that allow water to drain out the stern when opened.

Fairleads – A device to guide a line, rope or cable around an object. A fairlead can also be used to stop a straight run of line from vibrating or rubbing on another surface. An additional use on <u>boats</u> is to keep a loose end of line from sliding around the deck

Figure Eight Knot – General purpose stopper knot.

Floatation Device – Safety equipment to never be without

Foot of the Sail - The bottom edge or lowest part of a triangular or three sided sail,

Forestay - A wire or sometimes rod, that gives support for the mast, running from the bow or foredeck to a point at or near the top of the mast. Standing rigging that keeps the mast from falling backwards.

Fractional Rig - A design in which the forestay does not go to the very top of the mast, but instead to a point 3/4~ 7s, etc., of the way up the mast.

Freeboard – The distance or area that is between the deck or rail and the waterline. Most often it will vary along the length, size, and design of the boat.

Gooseneck - The fitting that connects the boom to the mast.

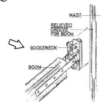

Grommet – An eye in the sail in which to pass a rope

Head of the Sail - The very top portion of a three sided sail.

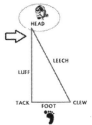

Header – If you are on a starboard tack and the wind shifts to the left, than you are headed, you simply can't sail as high.

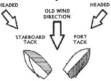

Heeling Over – Heeling is where a vessel tips sideways to some extent. The term is usually used in connection with the lean caused to a sailboat by the wind's force on the sails.

Hiking Out – The action of moving the crew's body weight as far to the windward side as possible, in order to decrease the extent the boat heels

Inspection Plate - A watertight round covering, usually small, that may be removed so the interior of the hull can be inspected or water removed.

INSPECTOR PLATE

Irons – Going directly into the wind.

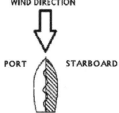

Jib Car – A pinstop slider that allows easy movement for sail trim and allows you to change the sheeting angle of the jib so the jib has a more efficient shape

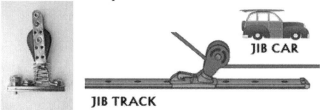

Jib Furler – A method of storing a sail usually by rolling the jib around the headstay

Jib Halyard - A jib halyard is a line that is used to hoist the jib sail.

Jib Sail - A jib is a triangular three sided sail that is located forward of a mainsail and mast of a sailboat.

Jib Sheet - The line used to trim the jib sail who's main function is to control the angle of attack on the wind.

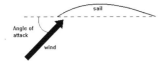

Jib Track – A track that allows a jib car easy movement to adjust and trim a sail

Jibe - Jibing a sailboat is having the mainsail go from one side of the boat to the other side turning with the wind behind you.

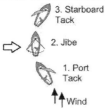

Knot – Boat speed and distance.

1 knot = 1 nautical mile per hour = 6076 feet per hour
1 mph = 1 mile per hour = 5280 feet per hour

5 Knots = 5.8 MPH	25 Knots = 28.8 MPH
10 Knots = 11.5 MPH	30 Knots = 34.6 MPH
15 Knots = 17.3 MPH	35 Knots = 40.3 MPH
20 Knots = 23.0 MPH	

Layline – Lines upon which you can sail close hauled or less and make it around the mark.

Leech – The outside aft or trailing edge of a three sided sail running from the head of the sail to the clew

Leech Tails – Essential guide for proper sail trim. Adhesive patches that bond to sail for high-resolution visibility

Lift – As the air tries to move from high pressure to low pressure it exerts a force on the sail; this force is known as lift.

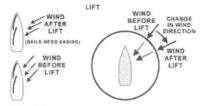

Link Tang Plate - A metal plate that may be attached to the hull to which the forestay or shrouds can be attached.

Locking Ring – Secures the clevis pin to the standing rigging via the link tang plate.

Luff of the Sail - The forward edge of a triangular or three sided sail. On a mainsail the luff is that portion that is closest to the mast.

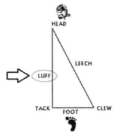

Main Halyard - The line used to raise the mainsail up the mast

Main Sheet - The line used to pull in and trim the mainsail whose major function is to control the angle of attack on the wind.

Mainsail – A sail located behind the main mast of a sailboat.

Marks – Inflated anchored course indicators.

Mast - Is a tall, vertical spar, or near vertical, spar, or arrangement of spars, which support the sails and rigging.

Mast Cleat – Wooden or metal fitting on the mast usually with two projecting horns around which a rope may be made fasten.

Mast Step - Fitting or construction into which the base of the mast is placed and secured to the boat.

Masthead Rig – A boat consisting of a forestay and backstay both attaching to the top of the mast.

Outhaul - Usually a line or tackle, an outhaul is used to pull the clew of the mainsail towards the end of the boom, thus tightening the foot of the sail. This controls the size of the draft in 40% of the mainsail by simply pulling in the clew.

 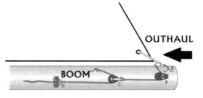

Pad Eyes – A small fitting with a hole used to guide a line.

Painter (or) Bow Line - The bow line or painter is a line that is tied to front or bow of the boat. It can be used to tow the boat or tie it to the dock. In the picture below it is used to secure the front of the boat to the boat dolly so the hull stays in place. This line can be used to tie the boat at the dock or be towed.

Pennie - Team shirt or bib that goes over a life jacket to identify a school or team when racing. *Goes over the life jacket.*

Pinching – Going too close to the wind

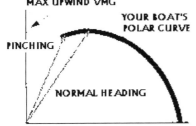

127

Pintle – A medal bracket that holds and attaches the rudder to small boats.

Port – The left side of the boat.

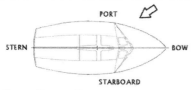

Port Rounding – Mark stays on the left or port side of the boat going around a mark

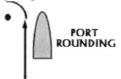

Port Tack – Wind filling the sail on the port side.

Puff – Wind that is coming to you off the water.

Rail - Also rubbing strake or rub strake. An applied or thickened member at the rail that runs the length of the boat and serves to protect the hull when alongside a pier or another boat

Rake - The fore or aft angle of the mast. Can be deliberately induced (by adjustment of the standing rigging) to flatten sails, and balance steering. Normally slightly aft

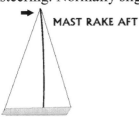

MAST RAKE AFT

Roach - The curved portion of a sail extending past a straight line drawn between two corners. In a mainsail, the roach extends past the line of the leech between the head and the clew and is often supported by battens.

Roller Furler – A device used to roll up a JIB sail for storage. Roller furlers are generally controlled by a line.

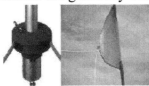

Roll Tack - Simply means using moveable ballast (i.e. the crew weight) to assist the boat in turning through the wind.

Rub Rail - Also rubbing strake or rub strake. An applied or thickened member at the rail that runs the length of the boat and serves to protect the hull when alongside a pier or another boat

Rudder – A rudder is a device used to steer a boat through the water. The rudder is attached to the stern of small boats using the pintal.

Running – When the wind is coming from directly behind the boat

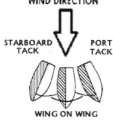

Sandbox – The starting area before a race.

Sawhorse - A simple small sawhorse placed under the front of the boat dolly will raise the bow and lets any water drain out the back.

Shackle – A shackle is a U shaped piece of metal secured with a clevis pin or bolt across the opening, or a hinged metal loop secured with a quick release locking pin mechanism.

......SHACKLE PIN

Sheets - Lines or ropes used to control the position of a sail.

Shrouds – Standing rigging that holds up the mast one shroud on each side of the boat, usually of wire or a metal rod.

Snap Shackle – Is a fast action fastener which can be implemented single handedly. It uses a spring activated locking mechanism to close a hinged shackle, and can be unfastened under load.

Spinnaker – A sail designed for sailing off the wind. A spinnaker is a large, triangular sail, most often symmetrical, flown from the mast in front of all other sails and the forestay. Used for sailing downwind.

Spinnaker Pole – Is a spar used to help support and control a spinnaker

Spreaders - Short horizontal spar extending from the mast to the shrouds of the boat to deflect the shrouds and allow better support of the mast.

Square Head Sail - The shape of the head of a mainsail.

Square Knot – Knot used for securing non-critical items.

Standing Rigging - Permanent rigging used to support the spars. Standing rigging may be adjusted during racing.

Starboard – The right side of the boat

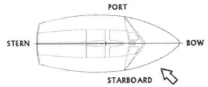

Starboard Rounding – Mark stays on the right side or starboard side of the boat.

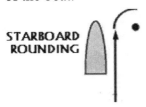

Starboard Tack – Wind filling the sail on the starboard side.

Stern - The aft portion of the hull.

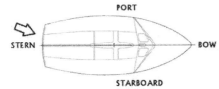

Tack - On a triangular sail, the bottom forward corner.

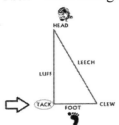

Tacking – Turning the boat so that the wind exerts pressure on the opposite side of the sail. Changing course going into the wind

Wind

3. Port Tack

2. Passing through the eye of the wind.

1. Starboard Tack

Teltails - Used to show direction of the wind. Located on the main or jib.

Tiller - The part of the boat that extends from the rudder to control steerage

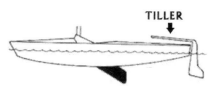

TILLER

Tiller Extension - A tiller extension allows the helmsman to hike out on the boat while still having control of the tiller and rudder. The tiller extension attaches to the tiller.

Track Stop – A device to stop a jib car on a jib track.

Transom - The flat or sometimes curved terminating structure of the hull at the stern of a boat.

Trapeze - Wire gear enabling a crewmember to place all of his weight outboard of the hull, thus helping to keep the boat level.

Triangle Course – Start to the windward mark than off the wind to downwind and to finish.

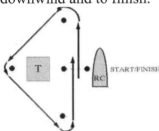

Traveler - A fitting across the boat to which sheets are led. In many boats the traveler may be adjusted from side to side so that the angle of the sheets can be changed to suit conditions.

Turtling – This is when the boat capsizes and the mast is pointed straight down.

Vang - A device, usually with mechanical advantage, used to pull the boom down, flattening the sail.

Whisker Pole - A spar attached to the mast and sail to help extend and spread out the jib.

Whistle Starts – The starting sequence before some races.

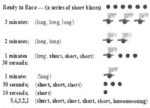

Winch - A winch is a mechanical device that is used to pull in or let out the "tension" of a rope or wire rope.

Winch Handle – Handle that is used to rotate and turn the winch.

Wind Direction Tools – Tie on the shrouds for wind direction.

Windex – Mounted on the top of the mast to show wind direction.

Window on Sail - A transparent portion of a jib or mainsail to look through

Windward Leeward Race Course – Start to the windward mark and to the downwind mark to finish.

Wing on Wing - This is simple. When you're going downwind your mainsail is on one side of the boat and your jib sail is on the other side.

ABOUT THE AUTHOR

I was the racing coach at Arizona State University sailing team. In 1990, I organized the Betsy Ross America's Cup campaign as a potential defender of the 1992 America's Cup in San Diego, California. It was the very first America's Cup team to name women crew member onboard. I also competed in the Olympic Sailing Trials in the Star Class in 1988. I have spoken at many clubs and sailing functions but teaching has always been my joy.

Born in Pasadena, California, I attended school in Los Angeles at the University of Southern California. Growing up, I spent my summers sailing and playing tennis on Balboa and Lido Islands by Newport Beach, California. My mother's sister, Rosemary, was Miss America in 1941 and had a summer house on Lido Island where I spent my days sailing and eating frozen bananas. Not necessarily in that order.

I would leave early in the morning and come back when it was time for dinner. I always loved sailing, but I had to drive the boat. Luckily, I always had friends who had sailboats and they let me drive. Tennis became a part of my life as well, and I ended up playing tournaments both in the U.S. and Europe.

At eighteen I got my pilot's license, which launched a thirty-five-year career with the airlines. First I flew with TWA (Trans World Airlines), then with PSA (Pacific Southwest Airlines), and finally with USAir. While with PSA and USAir I was in operations, doing weight and balances. I loved load planning and working with numbers. Sailing and flying go hand-in-hand. The thrust, drag, lift, and weight are so similar that I found it an easy learn.

Sailing and flying are just numbers, weather conditions, and geometry.

Learn everything you can about the boat you sail. You must be **ten times better than your competition to win**. You just have to want it more than the other guy and you will win. Big Time!

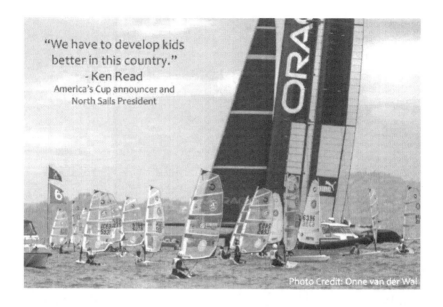

"We have to develop kids better in this country."
- Ken Read
America's Cup announcer and
North Sails President

Photo Credit: Onne van der Wal

O'pen BIC skipper Wilson Davis sharing some time with four-time Olympian Mark Reynolds at his sail loft in San Diego. Mark won two gold medals and a silver medal at the Olympics in the star class.

This book is dedicated to the
"San Diego Three"

Taisei Hatter - Jack Plavan - Jack Egan

&

Arizona's Wilson Davis

The future of Youth Sailing
It's all about Having Fun

141

O'pen BIC

2013-2014 Fall/Winter/Spring/Summer Event Calendar

There are now more than 100 sailing centers where O'pen BIC's are sailed, and some local fleets from Lake Geneva to Miami boasts more than 20 boats at casual fleet races. Nearly 200 kids participated at the 2013 O'pen BIC World Championship in Lake Garda, including 13 sailors from North America.

2013

November 16-17	Carlisle Classic – Clearwater Community Sailing Center / Clearwater, FL
November 23-24	Fall Harvest Cup – Miami YC / Miami, FL
December 7-8	Jr Olympic Festival – US Sailing Center Martin County / Jensen, FL

2014

February 8	O'pen BIC Show Down - San Diego, CA
March 1-2	Manning Regatta – ABYC / Long Beach, CA
APRIL 25-27	O'PEN BIC NORTH AMERICANS – Bermuda (charter boats available)
May 24-25	Memorial Day Regatta – ABYC / Long Beach, CA
June 2-6	Oshkosh Schools Sail Week – Oshkosh, WI
June 21-22	O'pen BIC Pacific Coast Championship / San Diego, CA
July 5-6	Jr Olympic Festival – Grosse Point YC / Grosse Point, MI
July 5-6	Great Lakes O'pen – Buffalo Canoe Club / Ridgeway, Ontario
July 12	Lake Geneva Prix O'pen Cup Un-Regatta – Lake Geneva, WI (TBC)
July 19th	Wisconsin O'pen Cup – Fon du Lac, WI
July 19-20	NSC Grand Prix O'pen Cup – Nepean Sailing Club / Ottawa, Ontario
July 19-20	Marblehead Junior Race Week – Marblehead, MA
JULY 25-26	O'PEN BIC WORLD CHAMPIONSHIPS – Travemunde, Germany
August 1	Vineyard Haven Un-Regatta – Vineyard Haven, MA
August 2-3	San Diego O'pen BIC Cup – San Diego, CA
August 7	Hyannis Youth Invite – Hyannis, MA
August 23-24	Columbia Gorge Un-Regatta – Cascade Locks, OR
September 13-14	Dinsmoor Trophy Regatta – Lahaina YC / Lahaina, HI

QUESTIONS
Contact: Philip Freedman at

info@openbiccalifornia.com

31663921R00089